Contents

Techniques	2	Mr & Mrs Gingerbread	34
Ewe and Me	22	Fruit Salad	36
Cup Cakes	24	Easy as Pie	38
Safari	26	Graffiti	40
Aquarium	28	Soap on a Rope	42
Delightful Ducklings	30	Café Latte	44
Pine for Me	32	Award Winner	46

Introduction

To use a scented herbal soap is to partake of an element of ritual used down the centuries. Since time immemorial, aromatic oils, perfumes and herbs have been used to cleanse, anoint and scent the body for hygiene, medicinal purposes, worship and spiritual well-being. Yet today, we take many of the toiletries we use for granted. We don't know how they are made or what goes into them. So why not create some lather in your life and discover the wonderful craft of soap making?

The latest ready-to-use 'melt and pour' soap bases are fast and easy to use, making it easy to craft, mould and shape fantastic vegetable glycerine soaps. Follow the easy step-by-step techniques and recipes provided in this book and you will be delighted with the results – deliciously scented, textured and colourful soaps that you can use to pamper yourself or give to friends and family.

2   Scented Soaps

Techniques

EQUIPMENT, SOAP BASE AND MOULDS

To make the recipes in this book you will not need any complicated equipment. In fact you will probably already have most of the equipment that you need in your kitchen. You will, however, need to purchase the raw ingredients to make your soaps.

These are easily obtained from the growing number of online soap supplies companies. They will usually sell most, or even all, of the ingredients and moulds that you will need to make soaps for craft and hobby use.

TO MAKE THE RECIPES IN THIS BOOK YOU WILL NEED:

- 'Melt and pour' vegetable glycerine soap base
- Plastic bowl, saucepan or double boiler for melting the soap
- Plastic or glass measuring jug or weighing scales
- Set of teaspoon and tablespoon measures
- Plastic or metal spoons or spatulas to stir the melted soap base
- Kitchen knife for cutting loaves of soap
- Cutting board
- Moulds
- Small spray or spritz bottle filled with surgical spirit or rubbing alcohol
- Colour (optional)
- Fragrance or essential oils (optional)
- Herbs, glitters, oils and additives (optional)
- Ladle (optional)
- Plastic tray or box lid lined with a plastic bag (only necessary when using cookie cutters or making swirls)
- Plastic food wrap or container to store the finished soaps

Techniques 3

SOAP BASES

All the recipes in this book use a pre-made vegetable glycerine soap base which is gently heated until it is liquid. This soap base is generally known as 'melt and pour' or 'melt and mould' soap. Liquid colour, herbs, oils, glitter and scent may be added to the melted soap base, which is then simply poured or cast into a mould. It is left to set until hard and is then ready to use. Melt and pour soap bases can also be artistically handcrafted by layering, swirling and embedding various objects. Setting times will depend on the thickness of the bar, the quantity of additives, the type of soap base and the temperature of the base and the environment.

There are several types of soap bases made by various large suppliers. On the right are details of some of the different bases you may find, and all good suppliers should be able to provide a full list of ingredients. Most of the following soap bases will have been made with coconut and palm oil, or derivatives of these vegetable oils, with added ingredients such as glycerine. Suppliers may also stock other bases including aloe vera, honey, shea butter and hemp. In humid or cold damp conditions, vegetable glycerine soaps may 'sweat' or attract moisture and 'low sweat' soap bases with reduced glycerine are sometimes available.

Basic/regular soap base	This is usually crystal clear and is ideal if you want to see embedded items, such as miniature soaps, pictures or other objects through the soap. It usually contains SLS (sodium lauryl sulphate), which may cause some skin irritation, but produces a frothy lather and has a good fragrance lift. It is also available in opaque white, which has added titanium dioxide.
Natural or SLS / SLES-free base	This has no added SLS (sodium lauryl sulphate) or SLES (sodium laureth sulphate) so should not cause skin irritation or affect sensitive skin. It is also usually free from surfactants or MPG (mono propylene glycol). It is a softer base with a slightly cloudier appearance than the regular clear soap base. It is very moisturizing and leaves the skin smooth and silky, but does not produce the same big lather as regular soap base.
Organic base	This is made from certified organic ingredients and is usually slightly yellow in colour. It is free from SLS and SLES, and does not produce the same big lather as regular soap base.
Olive oil base	This is translucent with a green tinge from the added olive oil and is softer than the regular base.
Goat's milk base	This has added goat's milk to moisturize.
Suspending base	This is useful if you want to suspend glitters, pumice, loofah, seeds, oats etc in your soap base.

4   Scented Soaps

FINDING MOULDS

Some of the household items used for moulds in this book:
- Empty margarine tub
- Plastic food container
- Flexible ice cube mould
- Tennis ball cut in half
- Plastic drawer tidy
- Yoghurt container
- Plastic plant pots (with the bases taped up)
- Empty crisp or potato chip tube
- Cardboard box or lid lined with a plastic bag

Many household objects or packaging from everyday life may be used as soap moulds. Any plastic mould may be used for making soap, as long as it has flexible sides to make removal easier.

Food packaging offers a wealth of suitable moulds, and next time you go shopping it will be hard to resist buying strange cheeses, unusual yoghurts and boxes of cookies just for their soap-moulding potential.

CAUTION
If you are using thin plastic food packaging as a mould, make sure the melted soap base is not too hot as it may melt or warp the plastic.

READY-MADE MOULDS

Moulds specifically designed for making soap are available from many different suppliers. Soap-making moulds are usually made with several different profiles on a sheet. As well as plain rectangles or heart shapes, you will also find many fun-themed moulds including animals, shells, stars or novelty items. Moulds made for chocolate-making are also suitable, and some of these are especially good for guest soaps or small soaps that can be embedded in translucent soap base.

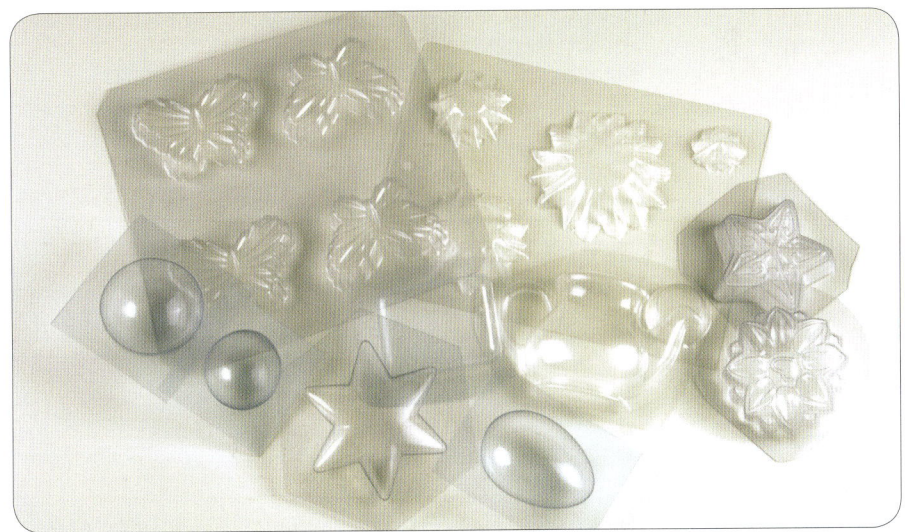

The basic soap recipe

Use this basic 'melt and pour' vegetable glycerine soap recipe to make all the individual variations on pages 22–47. When you have mastered it you can adapt it to make your own designer soaps.

INGREDIENTS
- 1 litre or 1kg (35oz) melted soap base
- 4 teaspoons essential oil or fragrance oil (2%)

Suggested additives (choose one or more)
- 1–2 tablespoons dried herbs
- 1 teaspoon clay
- 1 teaspoon mica or glitter
- 1–2 teaspoons oil, melted butter or Vitamin E
- 1 teaspoon honey or beeswax
- A few drops of liquid colouring

HOW MUCH SOAP BASE?
To work this out, simply fill your mould with water and pour it into a measuring jug. The amount of water in the jug will be the amount of melted soap you will need: 1 litre (1¾ pints) = approx. 1kg (2¼lb). If you overestimate, simply pour any excess melted base into a plastic tub to set. Melt and pour soap bases can be re-used several times over.

> **TIP**
> You may prefer to melt sufficient soap for several projects and ladle the liquid soap into the measuring jug as required. Do not leave the base on the heat for too long as the water will evaporate and the soap will become thick and coloured.

MAKING THE MIXTURE

1 Fill the mould with water and pour into a measuring jug (see 'How much soap base?' above).

2 Using a chopping board or work surface, cut the soap base into 2.5–5cm (1–2in) chunks using a kitchen knife.

3 Put the soap chunks into a large non-metal measuring jug (for microwave) or heavy-based saucepan (for hob).

Melting the base
Whether using a microwave or a saucepan on a hob, melt the base gently, until it becomes liquid, at approximately 160–165°F (70–75°C), depending on the base used. Do not overheat as the base may burn and become thick, cloudy or caramel coloured. It may also warp thin moulds.

4 Place the container in the microwave and heat on full power. Start with 20 seconds and continue in 10-second bursts until the base is melted, stirring between bursts. Stirring should disperse small chunks of soap left in the hot base without further heating. Take care not to get any of the hot soap on your skin.

Alternatively melt the soap base on top of the stove in a heavy-based saucepan or double boiler. Heat gently, stirring, until the soap is almost melted, then turn off heat and stir until the rest of the soap melts.

> **TIP**
> If using a microwave, the container should be considerably larger in volume than the soap base it contains to prevent spills.

ADDING EXTRA INGREDIENTS

5 Mix any powdered additives with a little water before adding to the base, to prevent clumping. See basic recipe for suitable additives and recommended quantities.

6 Melt additives like beeswax, hard oil or butters by heating gently in a saucepan or a metal jug on a hob. Stir gently to avoid creating bubbles in the soap. If using a jug with a metal handle (as shown), remember that the handle will be hot.

7 Combine additives with the soap base. Heavy ingredients may sink to the bottom, so allow the base to cool and thicken slightly before adding ingredients such as pumice, loofah or oats. If the base becomes too thick to pour, melt it down and start again. Additives may affect the colour or scent, so do not add colouring or fragrance at this stage.

ADDING FRAGRANCE

Soaps may be scented with essential oils (plant essences) or fragrance oils (scents made using synthetic aroma chemicals). The recommended quantity is 10–20g (2–4 teaspoons) of fragrance or essential oil to every kilo of soap base or 1–2% of weight. Do not add more than 3% fragrance or essential oil (30g per kg of base) as it may irritate the skin. It may also turn the soap cloudy.

8 Add the fragrance oil or essential oil, mixing in thoroughly to ensure even distribution. Do not add colour at this stage as some essential or fragrance oils contain a hint of colour that may affect the base. For example, adding blue colouring after a brown-tinted fragrance oil would produce a green-blue, rather than a blue soap base.

CAUTION
Use only skin-safe cosmetic fragrances for soap, never potpourri or candle fragrances. Mix in very thoroughly, as any concentrated areas of unmixed fragrance may cause skin irritation.

ADDING COLOUR

The easiest way to colour soaps is with cosmetic grade water-based liquid colour. Soap colours are usually very concentrated and half a drop may be all that is needed. Remember that the strength or dilution of liquid colour may vary from supplier to supplier.

9 Add the liquid colour drop by drop.

10 Stir in the colour thoroughly to ensure even distribution.

POURING AND SPRITZING

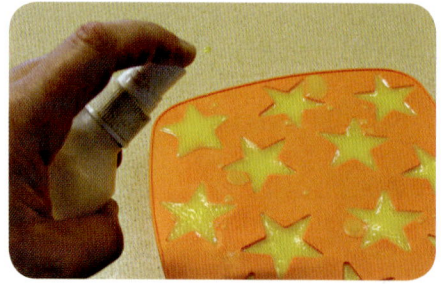

11 Make sure the melted soap base contains all the herbs, glitter, micas, oils, fragrance and colour that you wish to add. Pour into a plastic container or mould, or a container lined with plastic food wrap or bag.

12 After pouring, bubbles usually appear on the surface of the soap. These will set and spoil its appearance. Spritz or spray the bubbles with surgical spirit or alcohol to make them disappear as if by magic.

TIP
Before beginning to pour lots of small soaps, make sure the base is fairly hot or it may begin to set in the jug. Adding a teaspoon of water per litre/kg (1¾ pints/2¼lb) of soap will make the base more liquid and allow more pouring time. The excess water will eventually evaporate. Remember that you can always pop it back in the microwave to make it more liquid again.

COOLING AND UNMOULDING

Once you have poured your soap, leave it to cool. The time it will take to set will depend on the pouring temperature of the soap and the thickness of the bar. Small thin soaps or a soap sheet for rolls or swirls may be ready in 10 minutes, while soaps made in a loaf mould or margarine tub are best left to cool for several hours or overnight.

13 If using a rectangular mould, gently pull the sides away from the sides of the soap, turn upside down and gently press the mould until the soap pops out.

14 If you are using a shaped mould, turn upside down and gently press all around the top of the mould until the soap is released.

CUTTING THE SOAP

15 If you have made a loaf mould or large rectangular soap you may wish to cut it into individual bars. Cutting soap is similar to cutting through hard cheese. Any kitchen knife may be used, and it does not have to be particularly sharp.

16 The soap may also be cut using a soap cutter. These are available from soap making suppliers.

17 For an attractive effect, use a wavy potato chip cutter to cut the soap.

Further techniques

Melt and pour soap bases are very versatile. Once you have understood and perfected the various techniques, you will be able to create wonderful masterpieces of your own. These techniques will enable you to make all the recipes in this book.

LAYERING

1 Different colours of soap may be poured on top of one another to produce attractive layered effects. Pour the first layer and leave to set slightly so a skin forms on top. This must be set enough to hold the weight of the next layer and must still be warm.

2 Test the top layer with your finger; it should leave an indentation. Spritz or spray the first layer generously with surgical spirit to help the second layer stick or bind. Make sure the soap base is not too hot or it will melt the skin of the first layer and the layers will merge. Colour and pour the next layer. Repeat as required.

3 Leave the soap to set, and then cut the block into bars.

SWIRLING AND MARBLING

To make a marbled soap, swirl two different coloured soaps together. Make sure the soap base is not too hot (i.e. too runny), so the two colours marble together rather than merging into one colour. Pour the melted base into two different jugs, add a different colour to each, then pour both soaps at the same time. For a more marbled effect, use a wooden toothpick to swirl the colours.

ROLLS AND SHAPES

1 Add a teaspoon of water to every kg or litre (2¼lb or 1¾ pints) of melted soap base to make it more pliable. Pour the soap into a plastic tray or baking tray lined with plastic food wrap.

2 Leave to set until only just firm and pliable. If you wish, spritz with alcohol and pour on another thin layer of different-coloured soap to make a two-tone roll. Remove soap from tray. You may wish to cut and trim the edges of the rectangle to leave a clean edge.

3 Working very quickly, roll up the soap rectangle, or bend it into an S-shape. Cut the rectangle in half widthways, if too long.

4 Leave the soap roll or S-shape to set until hard, then spritz thoroughly with surgical spirit. Place in a clean cylindrical potato chip container or loaf mould. Pour in a contrasting colour soap.

5 Leave to set, then remove the roll carefully from the chip mould.

6 Cut the soaps. The overall effect should resemble a stick of seaside rock with the roll embed going right through the centre.

CAUTION
Make sure the soap is not too hot or it may melt the soap roll embed. The soap should be cool enough for you to be able to leave your hand on the side of the jug containing it.

MAKING A SCROLL

 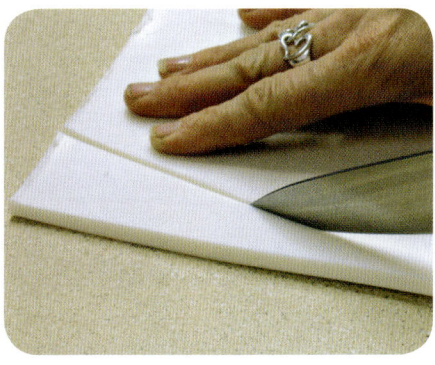 

1 Add a teaspoon of water to every kilo or litre (2¼lb or 1¾ pints) of melted soap base to make it more pliable. Pour the soap into a plastic tray or baking tray lined with food wrap. Leave to set until just firm but still pliable. Remove from the tray.

2 Make a tie to go round the scroll by cutting each side of the rectangle. Begin at the top, approximately 2cm (¾in) in and finish at the bottom edge so you have two very long triangles of soap.

3 Starting at the widest end of the soap, roll up into a scroll.

4 Cut a small nick in the widest part of one of the long, leftover triangles of soap.

5 Wrap the triangle around the soap and push the narrow end of the long triangle through the nick in the wide end.

The finished scroll. See page 46 for project

Techniques 11

COOKIE CUTTER SHAPES

1 Line a tray or cardboard box lid with a plastic bag or food wrap. Colour the soap, adding a teaspoon of water to every kilo or litre (2¼lb or 1¾ pints) of melted base to make it softer and easier to cut. Pour the soap into the container to a depth of approximately 1.5cm (½in), or the desired thickness to make a sheet of soap.

2 Leave to set until just firm, pressing a finger into the centre of the soap sheet to check consistency. Do not leave until completely cold as it will be harder to cut. Lift the soap sheet out of the container, remove the plastic wrap and place on a chopping board. Cut out your soaps using a cookie cutter.

3 Remove the soap shape from the cutter and leave to set until hard. Wrap with food wrap or place in a cellophane bag. Any leftover pieces can be melted down and used again.

EMBEDDING AND DECORATION

An embed is a small item embedded or buried in the soap, and a wide range of items is suitable. You can use any small soap made in an ice cube tray or small chocolate mould; small chunks of soap; soap swirls or soaps cut out with mini cookie cutters. Other ideas include stamps, coins, photographs, stickers, artwork, transfers, erasers, beads, ribbons or plastic toys.

1 Make or select suitable embeds. Pour a little soap base into the mould and leave for a few minutes for a skin to form.

2 Test the soap with a finger to make sure a skin has formed.

Alternative method
Fill the mould with melted soap and leave to set until a skin has formed on top and the soap in the mould has begun to thicken. Using the point of a knife or a toothpick, break the surface of the soap, spritz the embed and push it into the soap.

3 Spritz the bottom layer of soap with surgical spirit and place the embed on top, then spritz the embed. The surgical spirit helps to bind the soap layers and the embed.

4 Pour the next layer of soap on top. Take care that it is not too hot or the embed may melt. If you can leave your hand on the side of the jug, the soap base should be cool enough to pour.

CAUTION
Make sure any small parts used for embeds are kept away from small children and animals.

Scented Soaps

DECORATION

Soaps may be decorated by gently pressing in flowers or dried fruit when the soap it is just starting to set.

STORING SOAPS

If melt and pour vegetable glycerine soaps are left unwrapped in a cold or humid environment, their glycerine content will attract moisture and leave the soaps wet and slimy. To prevent this, wrap the finished bars in plastic food wrap or cellophane.

Do not leave soaps in direct light as their colour will fade very quickly, particularly if you have used powdered herbs to colour them. Soaps should be good to use for up to a year after making, sometimes even longer depending on the ingredients used.

REHEATING SOAP

Soap bases may be melted down several times, though some of the water content will evaporate each time. To prevent it becoming dry and brittle, add 1 teaspoon of water to each kilo or litre (2¼lb or 1¾ pints) of soap that you wish to re-melt. If soap that you are re-melting is fragranced, take care to allow for this before adding more fragrance. Too much may irritate the skin, and it is recommended that the finished soap should contain 1–2% of fragrance in total.

SELLING

The information in this book is to enable you to produce soaps for home use. If you want to manufacture products for sale, you should investigate fully the appropriate trading legislation of your country and of countries to whom you wish to sell. Most countries have strict legislation on weights and measures, manufacturers' details, batch numbers, record keeping, health and safety and insurances etc. In Europe bath products must also be certificated by a Cosmetic Chemist.

If you are giving soaps to a friend or family member, it is wise to label with the ingredients and store soaps and ingredients away from children and pets.

HEALTH AND SAFETY

Remember that melted soap is hot and can burn if it comes in contact with the skin. The skin and eyes must also be protected from neat essential oils. You may therefore wish to use protective clothing, gloves and goggles while making soap. If soap or any of the ingredients that you are using come in contact with the eyes, irrigate immediately with water. Label all ingredients and finished products clearly and keep well away from children and pets.

Troubleshooting

Making soap with melt and pour bases is relatively simple and problem-free. The following hints should help you to overcome the few problems that may arise.

Layers are not sticking together
Make sure you spritz the surface of the soap between each layer using surgical spirit or alcohol. Do not let a layer cool down too much before adding the next. When pouring another layer, the layer below should be warm with a skin on the surface of the soap.

Soaps will not unmould
Make sure soaps are completely cold and set before attempting to unmould them. If they will not come out, they may not be set. Leave them for a couple of hours or overnight, then try again. If you are in a hurry, place them in a refrigerator for a few minutes to speed up the setting process. Alternatively, slide the mould carefully along to a cooler part of the kitchen surface or table.

Soap embeds melting
Make sure the base is not too hot when pouring it on to a soap embed. Check also that the soap embeds are not too thin, or they may melt with the heat of the poured soap.

Embeds falling out of soap
Make sure that you spritz the soap embed fully and that the soap base you are pouring on to the embed is not too cool; experiment with different temperatures of soap.

Cloudy soaps
The soap base may have been overheated, heated too many times, or you may have added too much fragrance. Some 'natural' soap bases are slightly cloudy rather than crystal clear; if in doubt consult your supplier before ordering.

Bleeding colour
Most liquid colours will bleed into each other over time. To prevent this, non-bleeding colours are available from some suppliers.

Sweaty soap
The vegetable glycerine in melt and pour soap attracts moisture from the air, which in cold, damp or humid conditions can make it sweaty and wet. As soon as the soap has hardened and is dry to the touch, wrap it in food wrap or place in a cellophane bag.

Spots on soap
If little white dots appear on your soaps, the sugar crystals in the base may not have dissolved completely. This happens when the soap has not been heated to the required temperature. Some bases, particularly 'natural' types, have slightly higher melting temperatures, so check with the manufacturer when purchasing. Another reason may be that the soaps have been wrapped while damp: make sure soaps are dry to the touch before wrapping.

Discoloured soap base
If you overheat the soap base it may change to a brown or caramel colour with an unpleasant smell. Melt the soap base gently, and do not leave on the heat for long periods. The soap base may in theory be melted down several times, but for best results try to use it on the first or second time of melting.

Additives sinking to the bottom
Heavy additives such as pumice, oats or loofah may sink to the bottom of the soap if the base is too hot when pouring. Before pouring a base that contains heavy additives, stir it continually to cool and thicken it, as this will help to suspend the additives.

Ingredients

The basic techniques presented in this book will allow you to complete all of the recipes, but when you have gained a little confidence, they will also provide you with the ability to experiment and make your own soaps. To help you, this section provides useful information on some basic ingredients.

WARNINGS

- Essential oils must not be taken internally and must be kept away from children and animals. The recipes in this book are intended for those over the age of seven

- If you suffer from allergies, carry out a skin patch test before using your soap. Avoid exposure to sunlight or UV light for about 12 hours after using orange, lemon, grapefruit, bergamot, petitgrain, lime or mandarin oils

- Essential oils may damage clothing and wooden surfaces, so cover up before using them

- Do not use essential oils if you have high blood pressure or epilepsy; are receiving psychiatric or medical treatment; are taking homeopathic or herbal remedies; are pregnant or breast feeding; or wish to treat young children

ESSENTIAL OILS

Essential oils are fragrant, natural volatile liquids found in plant leaves, fruit, seeds, roots, wood, resin, gum, grasses and flowers. Plants release them in hot weather to protect against pests and infection or attract pollinating insects. They are antiseptic, and some are antiviral, antifungal and antibacterial. They are used in aromatherapy to help ease a multitude of complaints and conditions. They also affect mood and well-being, helping to relax both body and mind.

The complex chemical compounds contained in essential oils are thought to enter the bloodstream through the skin, and the oils are said to be a great help in easing a variety of skin conditions. A warm bath is one of the most pleasurable ways of using them. They must not be applied directly to the skin, however, and should be used in a carrier oil, bath bomb, cream or soap.

Lime

Mandarin

Techniques 17

PERFUME

Perfume is a blend of fragrant essences and oils obtained from flowers, grasses, resin, bark, gum, fruit, animals and aroma chemicals dissolved in an alcohol or oil base. Different combinations of these ingredients are mixed to produce varying strengths, such as eau de Cologne, eau de toilette and the most expensive eau de parfum. Perfumes can be used to scent creams, soaps, cosmetics and bath products.

Although the recipes in this book, list the essential oils needed for each soap, you can change them to suit yourself. In fact, blending essential oils to create your own fragrance for use in the recipes does not have to be a complicated process. It is possible to create a unique fragrance blend from just a few ingredients. But note that such perfumes should not be sprayed directly on to the body. As with all essential oils, they should not be used neat on the skin or in the bath.

If you want to use a specific aroma, you can buy ready-made fragrance oils. In this way, you will be able to scent your soaps with such delights as chocolate, apple, passion fruit, blueberry muffin, pina colada, mango and sea breeze. You can blend such fragrance oils together to create different scents. For example, several fruity fragrances could be used to create a 'fruit salad' fragrance.

HERBS AND BOTANICALS

Herbs and other plants provide a range of fragrant and therapeutic ingredients that can be added to your soaps: for example, leaves, flowers, seeds and berries (either fresh, dried or in powdered form). In creating your own soap, you may decide to take inspiration from the shape of your mould, treat a particular ailment or simply create a relaxing favourite fragrance. Don't overdo it, however. Sometimes, a simple transparent soap with a single herb or essential oil can be just as pleasurable as one jam-packed with lovely ingredients.

18   Scented Soaps

COLOUR

Of course, a clear or white soap base can be left uncoloured. Colour can play an important role in our lives, however, affecting our mood and sense of well-being. Some colours can relax and calm, while others can stimulate and revive. Visualizing colour can also affect the sense of smell.

There are various ways to colour soaps. Remember that the base colour may be affected by essential oils, fragrance and additives, so always add the colour at the last stage. You can add liquid cosmetic colour, coloured pigments, micas, natural herbs or spices, or clays.

The easiest cosmetic colours for use in soaps are liquid cosmetic colours. For the recipes in this book, you will need cosmetic grade liquid blue, red, yellow and green. Some liquid colours may bleed into the next colour or into the soap base, but non-bleeding colours are available from soap suppliers. These colours can be blended together to create different shades (see chart overleaf). If you have nothing else available, you can use liquid food colouring, but this is not always reliable and may fade quite quickly.

Simply add the liquid colour drop by drop until you achieve the required colour. Stir the soap thoroughly to ensure that it is mixed well. Alternatively, stir slightly to achieve a marbled effect.

Clays and powdered herbs and spices are a great way to add natural earthy colours. Mix the powdered ingredients with a little water before adding to the soap base to prevent the powder from clumping. Some ingredients may react with the soap base, fragrance or oils and affect the overall colour of the soap, so it is best to experiment first until you have achieved the desired colour. The recommended quantity is up to one tablespoon of powder per kilogram or litre (2¼lb or 1¾ pints).

Pigments are powdered colours made up of small particles. Choose varieties developed for the cosmetics industry, which will be safe and non-toxic. Pigments are strong and dense, and generally do not fade as fast as liquid colours; a tiny amount goes a very long way. As they are made up of fairly large particles, they are not suitable for clear soaps, but may be used for opaque soaps with a rustic look. Mix with a little water before adding to the soap base to prevent clumping.

There are also many cosmetic glitters and micas that can add colour and sparkle to your soaps. Note that only cosmetic-grade glitters can be used. Simply sprinkle them into the soap base and stir. To prevent them from sinking, keep stirring until the soap cools and thickens a little, then pour into the mould.

Mica powders are very fine particles that can add a beautiful pearlescence or iridescence. Mix with a little water before adding to the soap base to prevent clumping.

Cosmetic liquid colours can be blended to create your own shade. Below is selection of liquid colours available from soap-making suppliers.

CAUTION

- If you are using glitters in soaps remember that they should be kept away from the eyes

- Colours and their strength may vary from supplier to supplier, so use a colour sparingly the first time until you get used to its intensity and behaviour

- Remember that natural ingredients are just that: natural ingredients. Some can fade quite quickly. Do not leave soaps or ingredients in direct sunlight as it may destroy fragrance and colour

- The 'raw' colours are strong and intense and only a little is needed. It is wise to cover clothing and work surfaces when handling colour and wash any areas of contact straight away to avoid staining

Techniques 19

COLOUR MIXING CHART

You need to allow for the actual colour of the essential oils, fragrance or additives such as herbs or oils, which may change the colour of the finished soaps.

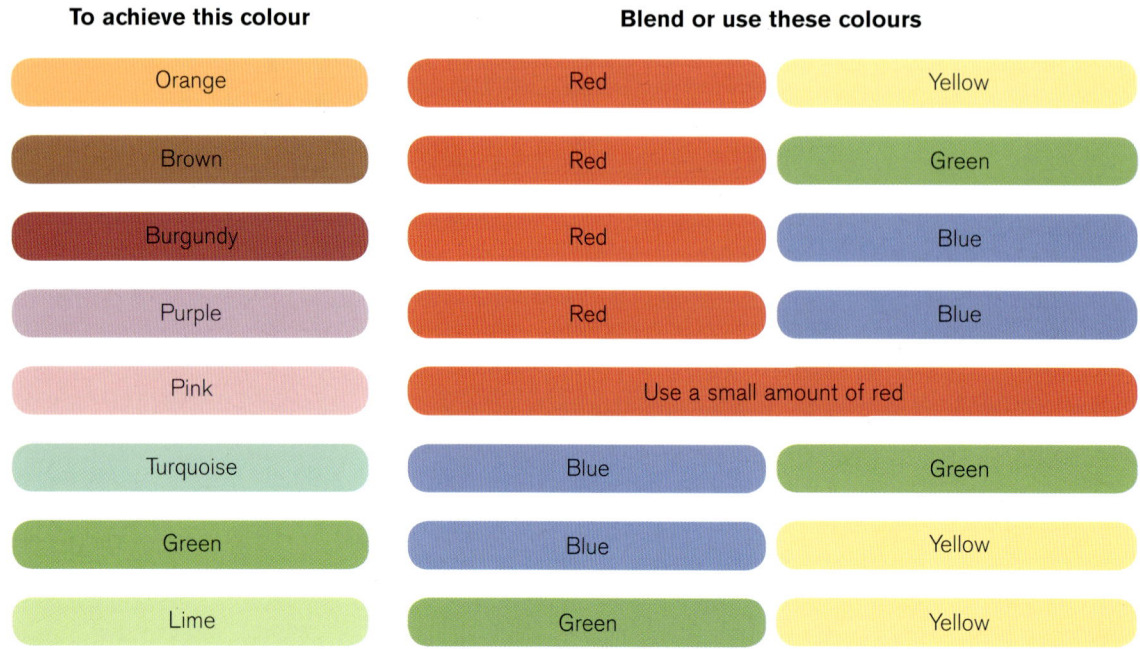

To achieve this colour	Blend or use these colours	
Orange	Red	Yellow
Brown	Red	Green
Burgundy	Red	Blue
Purple	Red	Blue
Pink	Use a small amount of red	
Turquoise	Blue	Green
Green	Blue	Yellow
Lime	Green	Yellow

OILS AND BUTTERS

Most vegetable glycerine soap bases will be made from a combination of vegetable oils, usually coconut and palm oils, but a little extra precious oil or butter can be added, either for its therapeutic properties or to nourish, moisturize, soften or protect your skin. Take care not to add too much, however, as the soap might become too soft and the lather may be reduced. Add no more than a tablespoon of liquid oil or butter to a kilogram or litre kilogram (2¼lb or 1¾ pints) of melted soap base.

Ewe and Me

These soothing sheep should help promote a good night's rest and happy dreams. Place a few by the side of your bed and, if the calming scent doesn't send you to sleep, you can always count them!

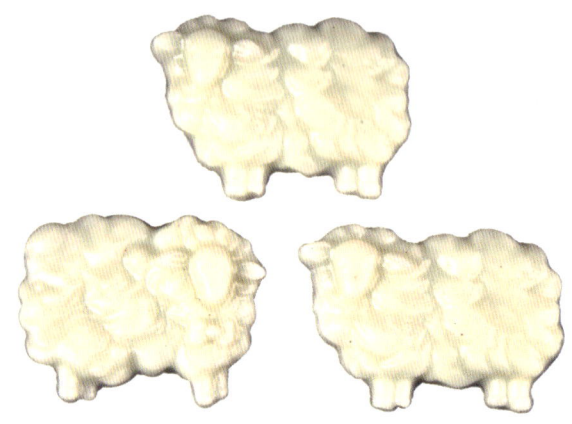

INGREDIENTS
- 1 litre or 1kg (35oz) melted white soap base
- 2 teaspoon organic lavender essential oil
- ½ teaspoon yarrow essential oil
- 3 tablespoons sheep's (or goat's milk) powder blended with a little water

MOULDS
- Mini sheep guest bar moulds
- Sheep cookie cutter

ADDITIONAL INSTRUCTIONS
Add a teaspoon of warm water to the melted soap to enable them to be cut out more easily. Pour the guest moulds first, then fill a plastic-lined tray with the remainder of the mixture and cut out the soaps using the cutter while still soft.

See pages 6–8 for basic soap recipe instructions.

OTHER IDEAS

Alternative fragrances:
Suitable alternative fragrances include mandarin or chamomile essential oil.

Cup Cakes

Get your chocolate fix without putting on a single ounce with these cute cup cakes. Full of antioxidants and skin-soothing properties, the only problem is that they are so pretty you won't want to use them.

INGREDIENTS
For the soap cherries
- A little clear soap
- A few drops of red colouring

For the 'chocolate' soap base
- 250ml or 250g (9oz) melted white soap base
- 2 teaspoons organic fair trade cocoa powder (blended with a little water)
- 1 teaspoon vanilla extract essential oil
- 1 teaspoon melted cocoa butter

For the topping
- 250ml or 250g (9oz) melted white soap base
- A few drops red liquid colour
- 1 teaspoon chocolate fudge fragrance oil

MOULDS
Silicone fairy cake/muffin moulds or fairy cake soap moulds

ADDITIONAL INSTRUCTIONS
Soap cherries: colour a little clear soap red, pour into a container and leave to set for a few minutes. While still pliable, take small pieces and shape them into small rounds. Leave until required.
'Chocolate' soap base: make up, then pour into the bottom half of the moulds and leave to set for a few minutes.
Topping: tint the mixture pink with a few drops of red colouring. Pour onto the chocolate base and leave to set for 5 minutes. Spritz the cherries with surgical spirit and gently press onto the cakes.

See pages 6–8 for basic soap recipe instructions.

CAUTION
Keep those soaps well away from young children who might decide they look good enough to eat.

Safari

Let your imagination take a road trip with this safari-themed soap bar that makes great use of children's fun erasers. The same technique may also be used with other mini-soap embeds.

INGREDIENTS
- 500ml or 500g (17½oz) melted clear soap base
- Children's fun erasers or other small items
- 2 teaspoons clear fragrance oil or essential oil

MOULDS
Any suitable mould

See pages 6–8 for basic soap recipe instructions.

CAUTION
Make sure the melted soap is not too hot before pouring over any small objects that may melt.

OTHER IDEAS
Many small objects can be embedded successfully in soap, including coins, photographs, stamps, erasers, charms messages, tickets and other memorabilia

Aquarium

Mysterious and wonderful things from the bottom of the deep blue sea are a fascinating showpiece for your embedding skills – you have to make the sea creatures and shells before you can embed them.

INGREDIENTS
- Tiny soaps for embedding

For the sea bed
- 200ml or 200g (7oz) melted white soap base
- 1 tablespoon pumice powder
- A few drops yellow colour
- 1 teaspoon Blue Lagoon fragrance oil

For the 'water'
- 300ml or 300g (10½oz) melted clear soap base
- A few drops of liquid blue or turquoise colour
- 1 teaspoon Blue Lagoon fragrance oil.

CAUTION
Take care when pushing embeds into the hot soap base.

MOULDS
Any loaf mould, margarine tub or food container

ADDITIONAL INSTRUCTIONS
Make a selection of embeds in various shapes including starfish, shells and tropical fish.

Make and pour the sea bed layer and leave for a few minutes to set slightly. Spritz the layer and place some small embeds on top.

Make up the soap base for the water. Spritz the small embeds, then pour in the clear blue soap mix, placing more embeds carefully as you go. If the embeds will not stand up in the molten soap, leave to set for a few minutes and then push them in from the top.

See pages 6–8 for basic soap recipe instructions.

Delightful Ducklings

These little soaps are a great incentive for reluctant youngsters to wash, and also double up as a bath toy – let your little ones go quakers trying to fish the duck out of the tub.

INGREDIENTS
For the duck
- 300ml or 300g (10½oz) melted clear or white soap base
- A few drops yellow liquid colour
- 1 teaspoon English Rain fragrance oil

For the pond
- 300ml or 300g (10½oz) melted clear soap base
- A few drops blue liquid colour
- 1 teaspoon English Rain fragrance oil

MOULDS
- Duck-shaped mould
- Round soap mould

ADDITIONAL INSTRUCTIONS
Make up the ingredients for the duck and leave to set until hard. Make up the ingredients for the pond, pour into moulds and leave until a skin forms on top of the soap. Using a knife or skewer, make a hole in this skin.

Spritz the duck, then place gently on top and leave to set.

See pages 6–8 for basic soap recipe instructions.

CAUTION
Can be used for age seven upwards.
Use less, or no fragrance, for younger children.

Scented Soaps

Delightful Ducklings 31

Pine for Me

Close your eyes and take an invigorating walk through an ancient pine forest fragrant with the scent of spruce, bark and earth. The aromatic oils will set you up for a day's work in the urban jungle.

INGREDIENTS
- 1 litre or 1kg (35oz) melted clear soap base
- 1½ teaspoons sandalwood essential oil
- ½ teaspoon cypress essential oil
- ½ teaspoon pine essential oil
- A few drops liquid green colour

MOULDS
- Stackable pine-tree chocolate-making mould
- Cookie cutters

See pages 6–8 for basic soap recipe instructions.
See page 12 for using tree-shaped cookie cutters.

Mr & Mrs Gingerbread

You're sure of a warm welcome from the Gingerbread family, with their spicy and comforting aroma. These make great gifts and are fun for children – just make sure they know they can't eat them.

INGREDIENTS
- 900ml or 900g (32oz) melted white soap base
- ¼ to ½ a teaspoon liquid orange colour
- ½ teaspoon ginger powder
- ½ teaspoon cinnamon powder
- 3 teaspoons ginger oil, or a spicy fragrance oil

MOULDS
- Mini ice cube or cookie mould
- Alternative: baking tray with cookie cutters

See pages 6–8 for basic soap recipe instructions.

CAUTION
Make sure these soaps are clearly labelled 'do not eat' and keep them away from children and animals.

Fruit Salad

This colourful zesty recipe is a summertime delight that is sure to be a favourite of children and adults alike, and everyone will want to take a slice home.

INGREDIENTS
For the fruit embeds
- Small quantity of clear soap base
- Red, yellow and green liquid colour

For the fruit bowl
- 1 litre or 1kg (35oz) melted clear soap base.
- 4 teaspoons Tropicana (or other clear fruity fragrance oil)

MOULDS
- Fruit-shaped ice cube moulds for embeds
- Plastic pudding basin or glass pudding basin lined with food wrap

INSTRUCTIONS
Colour small batches of clear soap base appropriately for each fruit (green for apple, red for strawberry, yellow for lemons etc). Make the small fruit embeds and allow to set.

For the fruit bowl, make the clear soap base. Spritz the fruit-shaped soap embeds, pour a little of the clear soap into the bottom of the mould and add some fruit soaps. Repeat until the mould is full.

If you do not have fruit-shaped ice cube moulds, use a plain ice cube tray to make rectangular coloured chunks. Plastic basins from ready-made steamed puddings are ideal for the fruit bowl.

See pages 6–8 for basic soap recipe instructions.

Easy as Pie

This one will really test your layering skills! The basic techniques in this recipe can be used to make all sorts of different pies, tarts or cakes, perfect for those who are watching their weight.

INGREDIENTS
For the fruit embeds
- Small quantity of white or clear soap base
- Yellow liquid colouring

For the bottom layer
- 200ml or 200g (7oz) melted white soap base
- 6 tablespoons oats
- 1 teaspoon lemon essential oil or lemon meringue pie fragrance oil

For the middle layer
- 200ml or 200g (7oz) melted clear soap base
- 1 teaspoon lemon essential oil or lemon meringue pie fragrance oil
- ½ teaspoon yellow liquid colour

MOULDS
- Lemon slice-shaped ice cube mould for the embeds.
- Flan dish or tin lined with plastic food wrap.

INSTRUCTIONS
Using the lemon-slice shaped mould, make the fruit embeds – colour soap yellow and leave to set.
Bottom: pour into mould, leave until set slightly, but still warm.
Middle: spritz bottom layer and pour on the yellow middle layer.
Top: whip the soap to create texture, spritz and pour. Quickly spritz lemon slices and push into the top layer.

See pages 6–8 for basic soap recipe instructions.

Easy as Pie 39

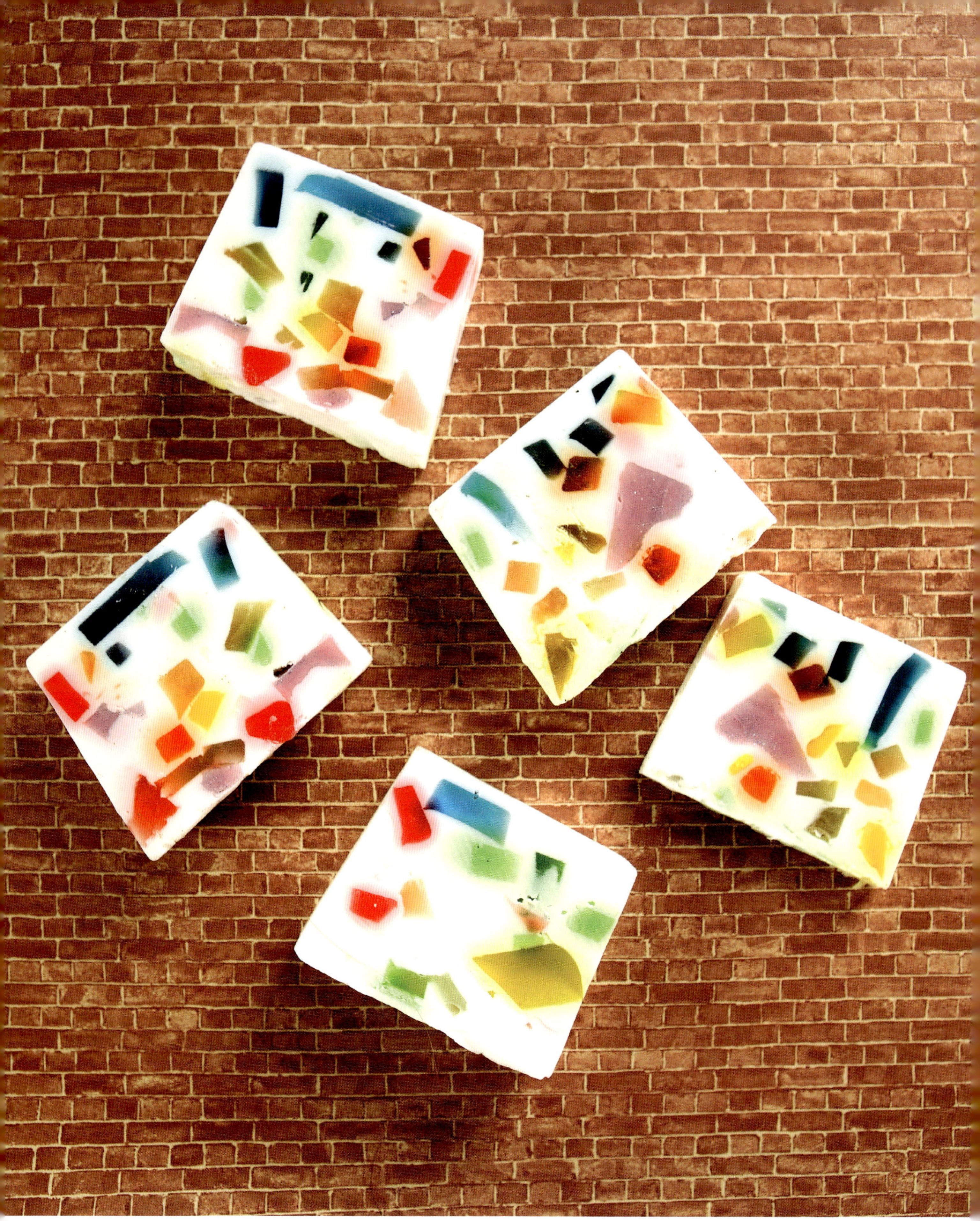

Graffiti

The writing doesn't have to be on the wall: focus your artistic urges on this wacky recipe that uses leftover pieces of soap. Go mad and throw clashing colours together to create a masterpiece.

INGREDIENTS
- 1 litre or 1kg (35oz) melted white soap base
- Multi-coloured soap scraps left over from previous projects
- 2–3 teaspoons fragrance or essential oil of your choice such as Cool Breeze

MOULDS
Any suitable plastic mould

ADDITIONAL INSTRUCTIONS
Pour some of the scented white base into the bottom of the mould. Chop up all the soap scraps and spritz with surgical spirit. Sprinkle the multi-coloured pieces into the white mixture. Pour in some more soap mixture, then add more scraps. Repeat until the mould is full for a fabulous multi-coloured confetti or graffiti effect.

See pages 6–8 for basic soap recipe instructions.

Soap on a Rope

Vegetable loofahs make an ingenious base for a soap on a rope to hang in the shower. Great for exfoliating the skin, they leave your body feeling silky smooth and healthy.

INGREDIENTS
- 1 litre or 1kg (35oz) melted clear soap base
- 2 loofahs with rope loops (available from chemists)
- 2 teaspoons lime essential oil
- 2 teaspoons lemongrass essential oil

ADDITIONAL INSTRUCTIONS
Wrap each loofah securely in plastic food wrap leaving the top part exposed. Place in a tray in case of leakage and pour the soap mixture into the top, making sure that the rope does not touch the soap. Leave until thoroughly set, then remove the food wrap.

See pages 6–8 for basic soap recipe instructions.

OTHER IDEAS
Use any other citrus oil such as lemon, mandarin, may chang, grapefruit, tangerine or clementine.

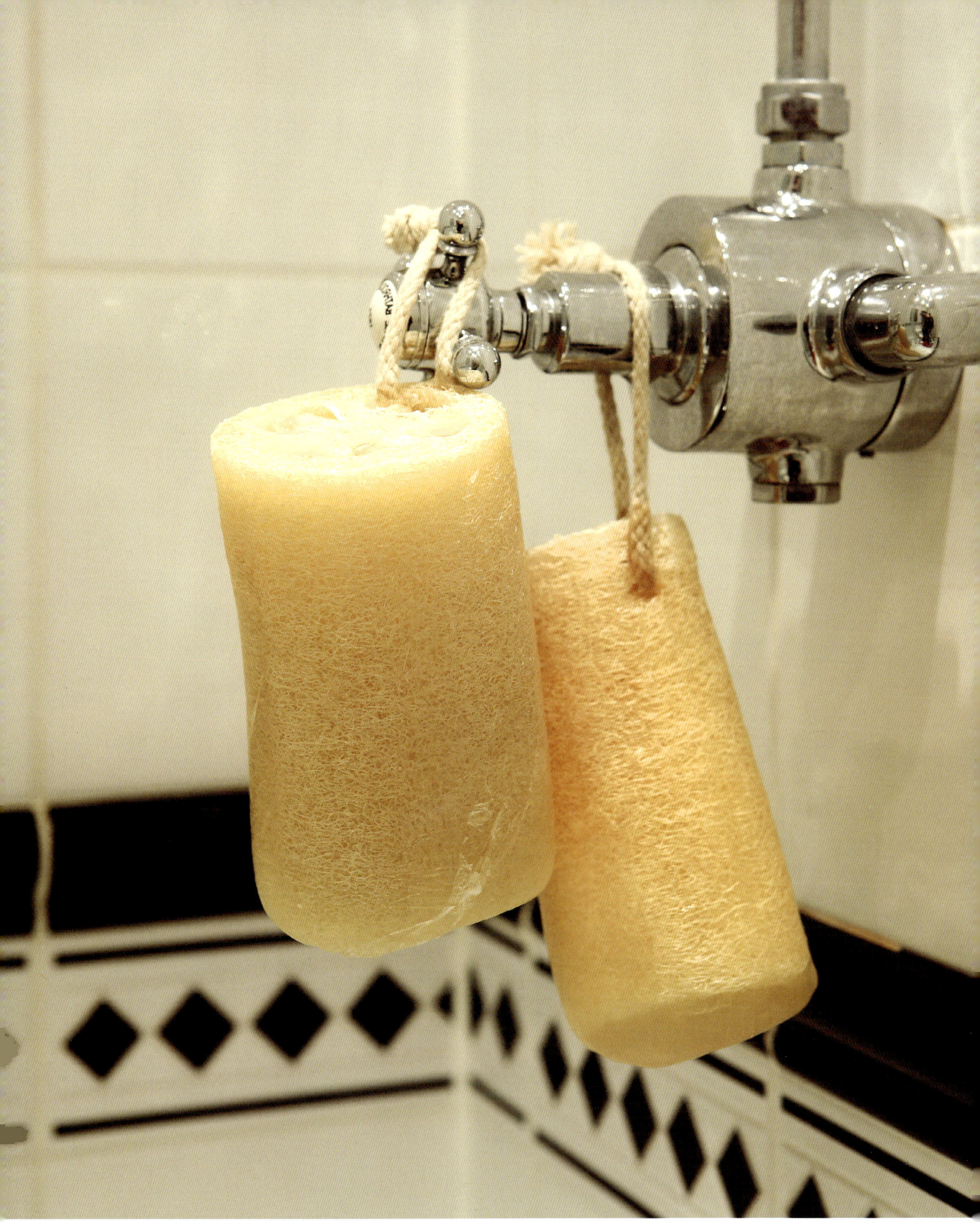

44 Scented Soaps

Café Latte

Coffee is said to be stimulating and full of antioxidants, so wake yourself and your skin before breakfast with a shot of caffeine in the shower. It's a great pick-me-up for tired skin after a late night.

INGREDIENTS
- 500ml or 500g (17½oz) melted white soap base
- 2 tablespoons milk or whey powder blended with a little water
- ¼ teaspoon organic fair trade instant coffee (blended with a little water)
- ½ teaspoon black coffee fragrance oil
- ½ teaspoon chocolate truffle fragrance oil

For the swirl
- 300ml or 300g (10½oz) melted white soap base with 1 teaspoon water added
- 1 teaspoon organic fair trade instant coffee (blended with a little water)
- 1 teaspoon of black coffee fragrance oil
- 1 teaspoon of chocolate truffle fragrance oil

ADDITIONAL INSTRUCTIONS
Make the swirl using the instructions on page 10. Spritz with surgical spirit and place inside a clean crisp/potato chip tube. Make the rest of the mixture and, when cooled, slightly pour into the mould around the swirl.

See pages 6–8 for basic soap recipe instructions.

Award Winner

Passed an exam? Reached a goal? Present this special soap scroll to a high achiever, or simply an all round-winner who deserves recognition. Make different-coloured layers and roll together for dramatic effect.

INGREDIENTS
- 500ml or 500g (17½oz) melted white soap base
- 2 teaspoons rooibos (red bush) tea
- ¼ teaspoon myrrh essential oil
- ¼ teaspoon frankincense essential oil
- ¼ teaspoon vetiver essential oil
- 1 teaspoon neroli light
- 1 teaspoon argan oil
- 1 teaspoon annatto powder
  (or ½ teaspoon liquid yellow colour)

ADDITIONAL INSTRUCTIONS
Pour the soap into a lined tray and leave to set until only just set and still pliable. Take out the sheet of soap and cut in half. Taper each rectangle (see page 11 for instructions) and quickly roll up into a scroll.

See pages 6–8 for basic soap recipe instructions.

Award Winner 47

48 Scented Soaps